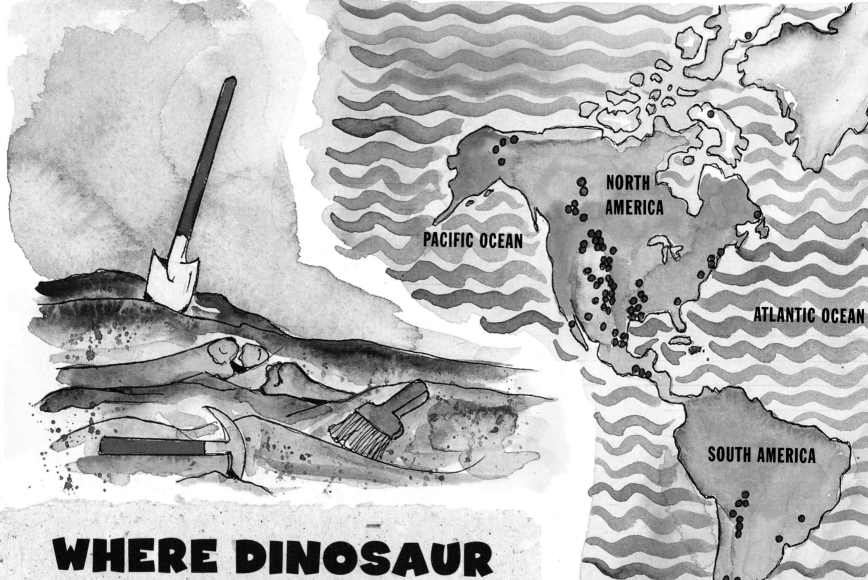

WHERE DINOSAUR
FOSSILS HAVE
BEEN FOUND

EUROPE

ASIA

AFRICA

PACIFIC OCEAN

INDIAN OCEAN

AUSTRALIA

To young paleontologists
past, present, and future

Special thanks to Carl Mehling of the
Department of Paleontology of The American
Museum of Natural History, New York,
New York, for reviewing the text.

Library of Congress Cataloging-in-Publication Data
Gibbons, Gail.
Dinosaur discoveries / by Gail Gibbons.
p. cm.
ISBN 0-8234-1971-1 (hardcover)
1. Dinosaurs—Juvenile literature. I. Title.
QE861.5.G53 2005
567.9—dc22
2004060701

ISBN-13: 978-0-8234-1971-5 (hardcover)
ISBN-13: 978-0-8234-2030-8 (paperback)

ISBN-10: 0-8234-1971-1 (hardcover)
ISBN-10: 0-8234-2030-2 (paperback)

AUTHOR'S NOTE

This book is about nonbird dinosaurs that lived on land between 230 million and 65 million years ago. These creatures shared the planet with other animals and sea creatures. Scientists piece together what they believe dinosaurs looked like from fossils that are millions of years old. Because they only have fossilized remains to study and use to reconstruct what a dinosaur looked like, there has been a lot of educated guesswork. In fact, it is still not known what colors dinosaurs were.

Crocodiles are the closest living relative to dinosaurs. Like today's crocodiles, dinosaurs had scaly skin, laid eggs, and had backbones. Today, crocodiles move about using legs that stick out away from their bodies. Dinosaurs stood with their legs beneath them.

Very few of all dinosaur fossils in existence have been discovered. Over time, scientists hope to discover thousands of new fossils and learn about other kinds of dinosaurs. Studying the world of dinosaurs will always be a process of discovery.

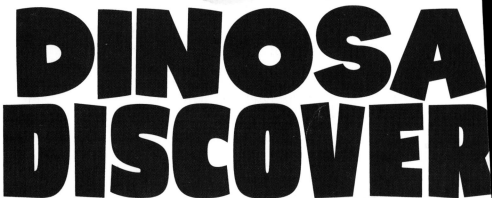

DINOSA
DISCOVER

by **GAIL GIBBONS**

HOLIDAY HOUSE / New York

UR
RIES

A **METEORITE** is matter that travels from space to Earth's surface and lands as a mass of metal and/or rock.

Triceratops
(try•SER•ah•tops)

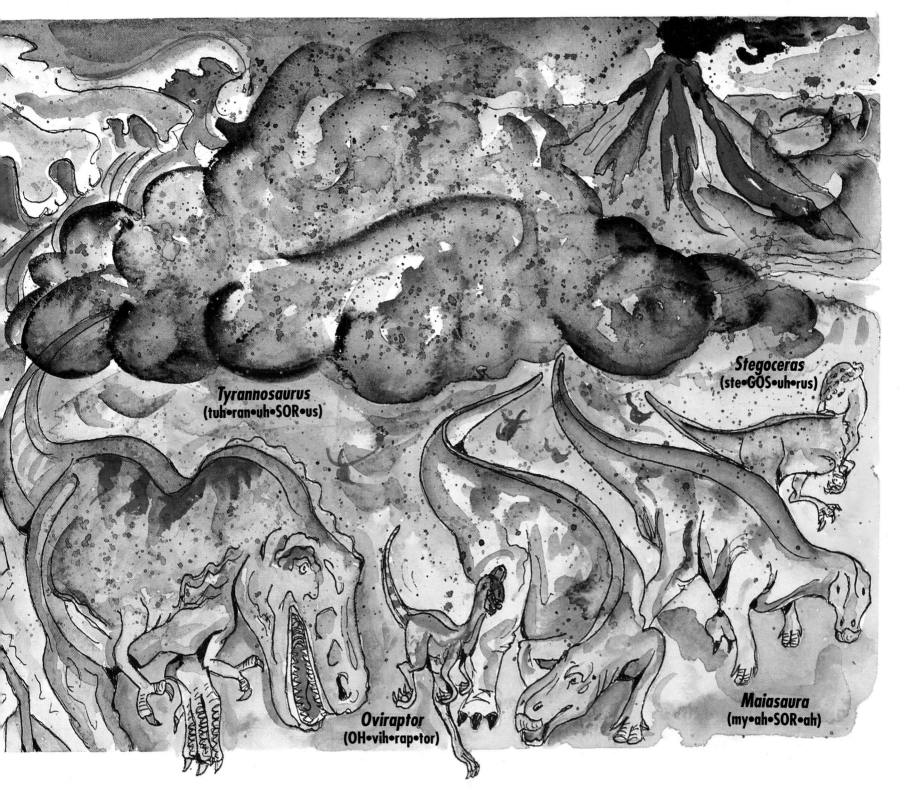

The **CENOZOIC ERA** (sen•oh•ZOH•ik) was after dinosaurs lived.

The **MESOZOIC ERA** (mez•oh•ZOH•ik) was when dinosaurs lived.

An **ERA** is one of three main divisions of geologic time.

A **PERIOD** is a part of an **ERA**.

— **CRETACEOUS PERIOD**

Some dinosaurs were gentle creatures and others were fierce attackers. Some were meat eaters, but most were plant eaters. They survived for 165 million years, between 230 and 65 million years ago. But the only way we know dinosaurs even existed is because of dinosaur discoveries.

— **JURASSIC PERIOD**

— **TRIASSIC PERIOD**

The **PALEOZOIC ERA** (pay•lee•oh•ZOH•ik) was before dinosaurs lived.

4

THE AG

CRETACEOUS (krih•TAY•shus) **PERIOD**
145 to 65 million years ago

Ankylosaurus (ang•kie•lo•SOR•us)

Protoceratops (pro•toh•SER•rah•top

JURASSIC (jeh•RASS•ik) **PERIOD**
208 to 145 million years ago

Kentrosaurus (ken•tro•SOR•us)

TRIASSIC (try•ASS•ik) **PERIOD**
230 to 208 million years ago

Mussaurus (mus•SOR•us)

OF THE DINOSAURS

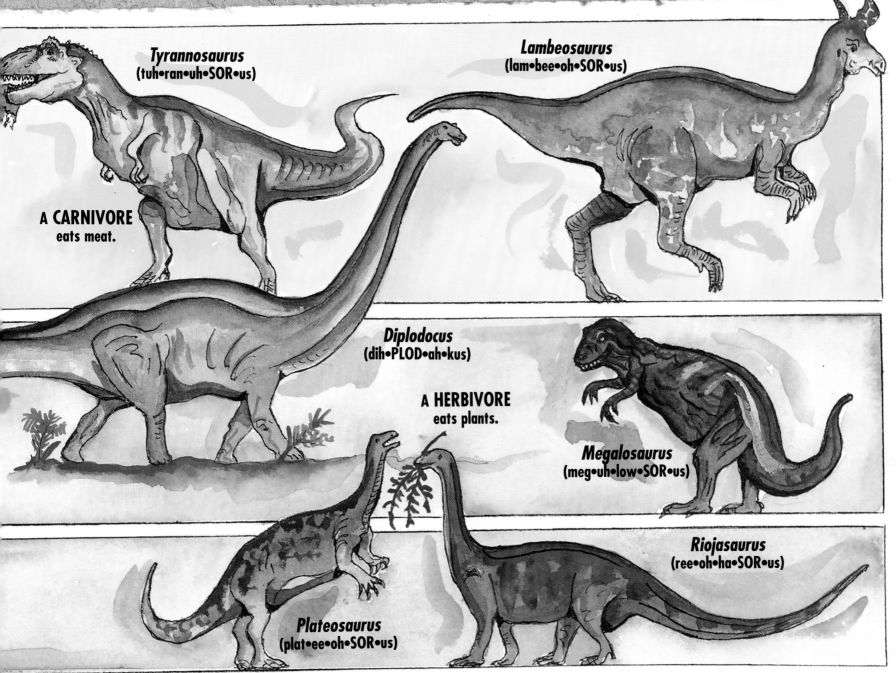

Tyrannosaurus
(tuh•ran•uh•SOR•us)

Lambeosaurus
(lam•bee•oh•SOR•us)

A CARNIVORE
eats meat.

Diplodocus
(dih•PLOD•ah•kus)

A HERBIVORE
eats plants.

Megalosaurus
(meg•uh•low•SOR•us)

Riojasaurus
(ree•oh•ha•SOR•us)

Plateosaurus
(plat•ee•oh•SOR•us)

The first fossils scientists determined to be those of a dinosaur were discovered in England in the 1820s. Dinosaurs died millions of years ago, and over time, sand, mud, and other materials covered them. Over many, many years, the bones of the dinosaurs turned into fossils. Dinosaur fossils have been found lying on the ground or embedded in earth or rock. Many dinosaur fossils have been found by amateurs, sometimes by accident. Other fossils have been found by paleontologists.

In 1842, Sir Richard Owen, a scientist, named the creatures whose fossils he was studying *dinosaurs,* which means "terrible lizard" in Greek.

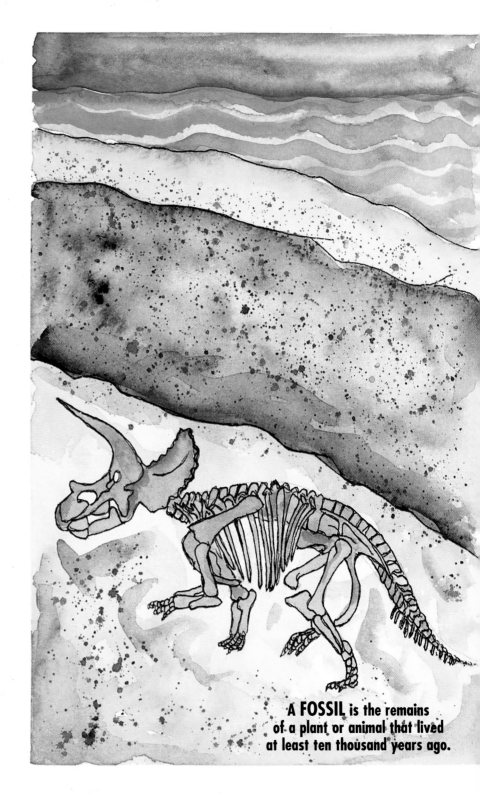

A **FOSSIL** is the remains of a plant or animal that lived at least ten thousand years ago.

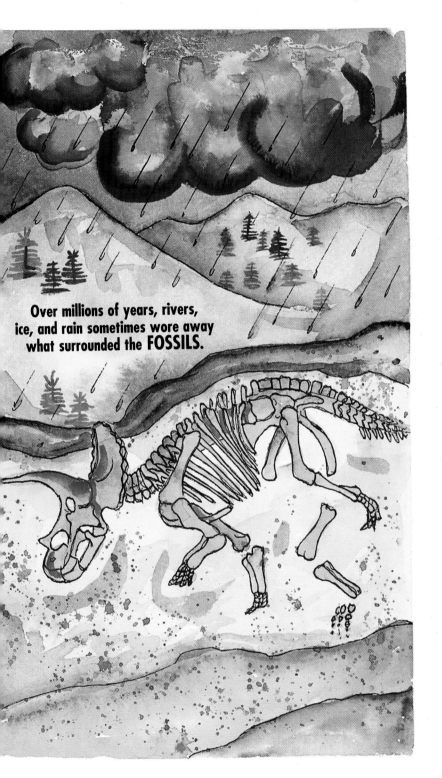

Over millions of years, rivers, ice, and rain sometimes wore away what surrounded the **FOSSILS.**

A PALEONTOLOGIST (pay•lee•on•TOL•o•jist) is a scientist who learns about ancient life by studying fossils.

The discovery of a dinosaur fossil is often an important event. Who knows? With each find, a new kind of dinosaur could be discovered. After the paleontologists arrive at the site, they record the date, time, and place of the find. Next, excavation begins. Fragile fossils, big and small, are removed using special tools. The fossils are sent to a laboratory or museum, where they are studied and the reconstruction of a dinosaur begins. The fossilized bones are assembled like pieces of a puzzle. Broken fossils are glued together. Next, people attempt to re-create missing pieces, muscle placement, and layers of skin, trying to figure out what the dinosaur looked like. From discovery to reconstruction can take years.

Natural history museums often have reconstructed dinosaur skeletons on display.

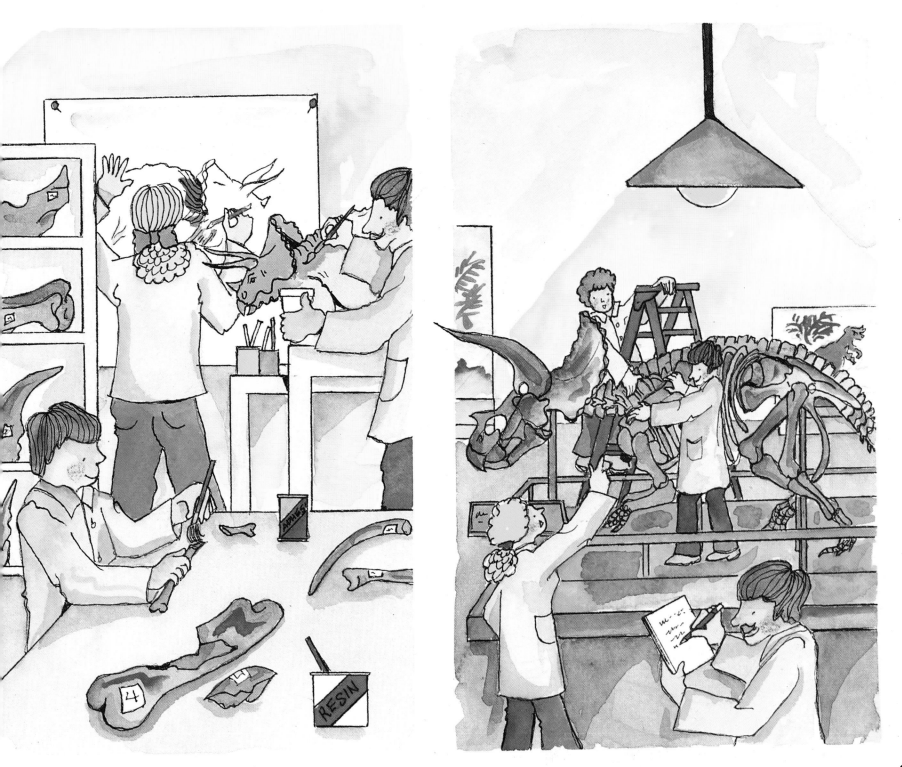

About one thousand different kinds of dinosaurs have been discovered so far. When a new kind of dinosaur is found, it is usually given a Latin or Greek name that describes what it looked like, or it is named after a person who found it or the place where it was found.

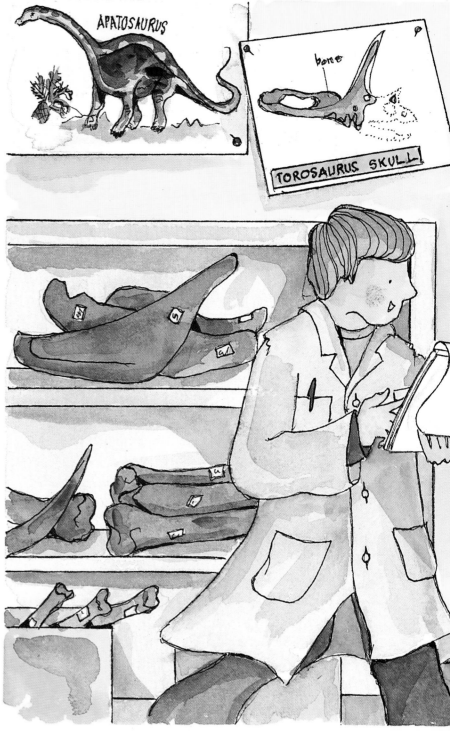

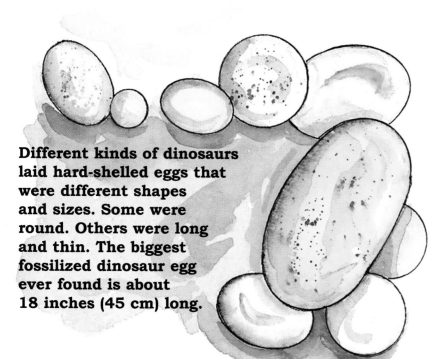

Different kinds of dinosaurs laid hard-shelled eggs that were different shapes and sizes. Some were round. Others were long and thin. The biggest fossilized dinosaur egg ever found is about 18 inches (45 cm) long.

11

PROSAUROPODS

(pro·SOR·uh·pods) were one of the earliest groups of dinosaurs.

Paleontologists have classified dinosaurs into different groups based on what their bones looked like. One of the earliest groups, prosauropods, lived during the Triassic Period. Most of them walked on all four legs. They had lizardlike heads, long necks, big bodies, and long tails. Prosauropods ate plants. Some of these early dinosaurs could stand on their hind legs to reach for leaves and branches on trees or to run from enemies.

Riojasaurus (ree•oh•huh•SOR•us) means "Rioja lizard." The dinosaur was named af[ter] La Rioja province in Argentina where it w[as] found. It was about 33 feet (10 m) long

Anchisaurus (ang•kee•SOR•us) means "near lizard." The dinosaur was named this because it lived near the beginning of the Age of the Dinosaurs.

Anchisaurus was about the size of a large dog.

12

Plateosaurus (plat•ee•oh•SOR•us) means "large lizard." The dinosaur was named this because it was a large animal.

Melanorosaurus (mel•ann•or•uh•SOR•us) means "Black Mountain lizard." The dinosaur's fossils were first found in the Black Mountains of South Africa.

Mussaurus (mus•SOR•us) means "mouse lizard." It was named this because the first fossil found of this dinosaur was of a small hatchling.

13

THEROPODS

(THEH·ruh·pods) were the group of meat-eating dinosaurs.

Theropods are another group of dinosaurs. All of these creatures stood on powerful legs. They had claws on their toes. When running, their long and stiff tails counter-balanced the weight of their huge heads and bodies. Most of them used their very sharp claws for killing their prey. Most often they used their long, sharp teeth and powerful jaw muscles to dig into the flesh of dinosaurs and other animals. Some theropods were small, fast hunters. Some would attack, using their sickle-shaped claws on their hind legs.

Dilophosaurus (die•low•foh•SOR•us) means "two-crest lizard." The dinosaur was named this because it had two bony ridges on its head.

Megalosaurus (meg•ah•low•SOR•us) means "big lizard." The dinosaur was named this because it was huge.

Compsognathus (komp•sog•NAY•thus) means "elegant jaw." The dinosaur was n[amed] this because the first fossils fou[nd] were beautifully preserved.

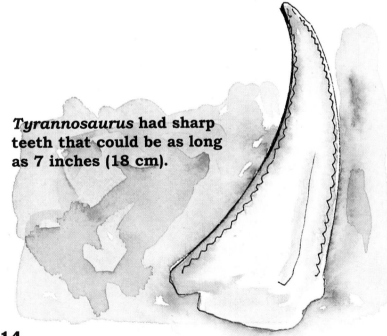

Tyrannosaurus had sharp teeth that could be as long as 7 inches (18 cm).

14

Giganotosaurus
(juh•ga•note•oh•SOR•us) means
"giant southern lizard." The dinosaur
was named this because it was a giant
dinosaur and was found in South America.
It was about 46 feet (14 m) long.

Deinonychus
(die•NON•uh•kus) means
"terrible claw." The dinosaur was
named this because both of its
feet had large hooked claws.

Tyrannosaurus
(tuh•ran•uh•SOR•us) means
"tyrant lizard." The dinosaur was named this
because it was a terrifying dinosaur. It is
sometimes called *Tyrannosaurus rex*.
Rex means "king" in Latin.

Velociraptor
(vuh•loss•uh•RAP•tor) means
"swift robber." The dinosaur was named
this because it could run fast.

Oviraptor
(OH•vih•rap•tor) means
"egg robber." The dinosaur was named
this because the first fossils to be found
were on top of a clutch of eggs that may
have belonged to another dinosaur.

SAUROPODS

(SOR·o·pods) were the largest of all dinosaurs. They were long-necked plant eaters.

Sauropods were the tallest and largest of all dinosaurs. They moved about on four legs that supported their enormous weight. They held their long tails off the ground to counterbalance their long necks. Some sauropods grazed in herds for protection. When predators appeared, some sauropods may have used their whiplike tails to make a loud, cracking sound to scare away their enemies. It is believed sauropods could live to be 120 years old.

JURASSIC

Camarasaurus (cam•uh•ruh•SOR•us) means "chambered lizard." The dinosaur wa named this because its vertebrae ha air spaces, or chambers, in them.

Brachiosaurus (brack•ee•oh•SOR•us) means "arm lizard." The dinosaur was named this because of its long front legs.

Apatosaurus (a•pat•oh•SOR•us) means "fraud lizard." The dinosaur was named this because some of its bones deceptively looked like those of another dinosaur.

Argentinosaurus was possibly the heaviest creature to have ever walked on land. It weighed as much as 100 tons (90 tonnes).

Diplodocus (dih•PLOD•ah•kus) means "double beamed." The dinosaur named this because of the dou row of bones inside its tail.

Saltasaurus
(salt•ah•SOR•us) means
"Salta lizard." The dinosaur was named after Salta
province in Argentina where it was found.

Argentinosaurus
(are•jen•teen•oh•SOR•us) means
"Argentina lizard." The dinosaur was
named for Argentina where it was found.
It was about 98 feet (30 m) long.

STEGOSAURS

(STEG·uh·sors) were the group of plated dinosaurs.

Stegosaurs had plates and spikes on their backs and tails. Some paleontologists believe the plates could have controlled the stegosaurs' body temperatures. Stegosaurs ate plants. When attacked, they may have swung their spiked tails at their enemies.

JURASSIC

PLATES

SP

Kentrosaurus had both plates and spikes on its back.

Stegosaurus (steg•uh•SOR•us) means "roof lizard." Paleontologists first thought th plates laid flat on the dinosaur's back, formin a "roof." It was about 30 feet (9 m) long.

Kentrosaurus
(ken•tro•SOR•us) means
"[spi]ked lizard." The dinosaur was named
[t]his because it had so many spikes.

Wuerhosaurus
(woo•err•ho•SOR•us) means
"Wuerho lizard." The dinosaur was named for
Wuerho, a town in China, where it was found.

ANKYLOSAURS

(ang·kie·lo·SORS) were the group of armored dinosaurs.

Ankylosaurs were heavily armored for protection from predators. Their bodies were covered with thick plates. Some ankylosaurs had spikes and some had strong tailbones with bony clubs on their ends. These creatures could swing their club-ended tails to whack any attackers. They ate plants.

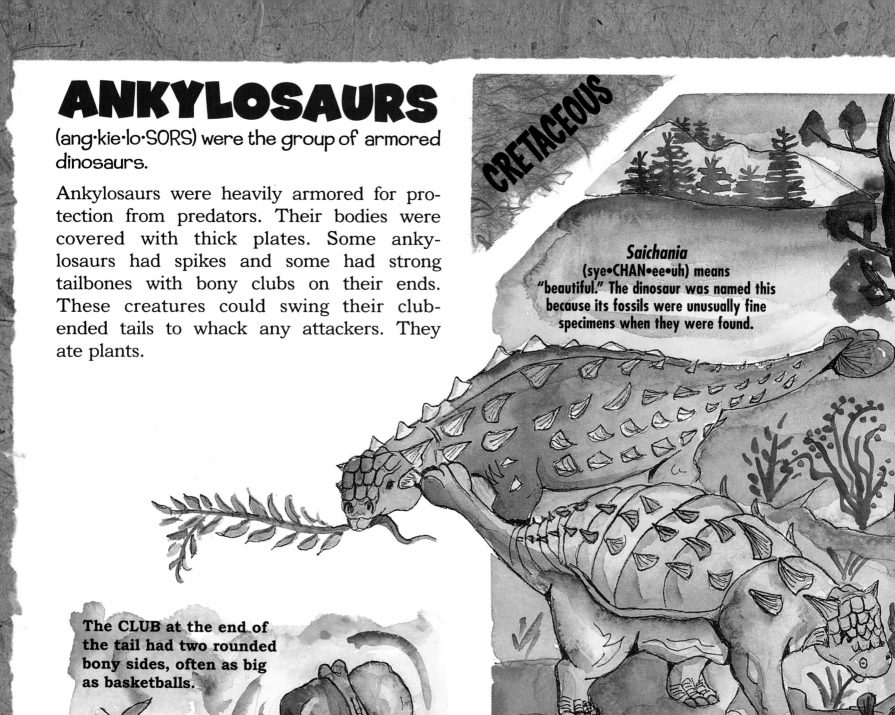

CRETACEOUS

Saichania (sye•CHAN•ee•uh) means "beautiful." The dinosaur was named this because its fossils were unusually fine specimens when they were found.

The CLUB at the end of the tail had two rounded bony sides, often as big as basketballs.

Euoplocephalus (you•op•low•SEF•ah•lus) means "well-protected head." The dinosaur was named this because it had a heavily protected bony skull.

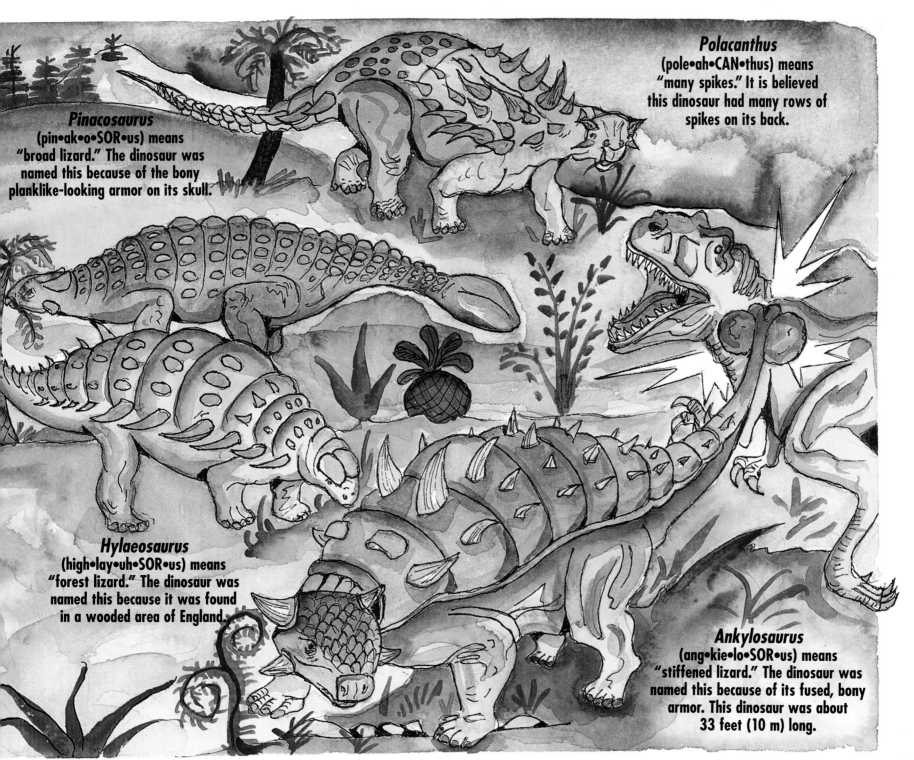

Polacanthus
(pole•ah•CAN•thus) means "many spikes." It is believed this dinosaur had many rows of spikes on its back.

Pinacosaurus
(pin•ak•o•SOR•us) means "broad lizard." The dinosaur was named this because of the bony planklike-looking armor on its skull.

Hylaeosaurus
(high•lay•uh•SOR•us) means "forest lizard." The dinosaur was named this because it was found in a wooded area of England.

Ankylosaurus
(ang•kie•lo•SOR•us) means "stiffened lizard." The dinosaur was named this because of its fused, bony armor. This dinosaur was about 33 feet (10 m) long.

21

CERATOPSIANS

(ser·ra·TOP·see·uns) were the group of dinosaurs often having large horns and heads with frills.

Ceratopsians had very thick skin and bony frills on the backs of their heads. Their horns were used as weapons. They were plant eaters that broke off plants for food using their strong beaks. It is believed they lived in herds.

CRETACEOUS

Pachyrhinosaurus (pack•eye•rine•oh•SOR•us) means "thick-nose lizard." The dinosaur was named this because it had a thick massive bone on its nose.

Torosaurus had the largest skull of any land animal that ever lived. Its skull was about 8 feet (2.4 m) long.

Pentaceratops (pen•tuh•SER•uh•tops) means "five-horn face." The dinosaur was named this because there were five horns on its face.

22

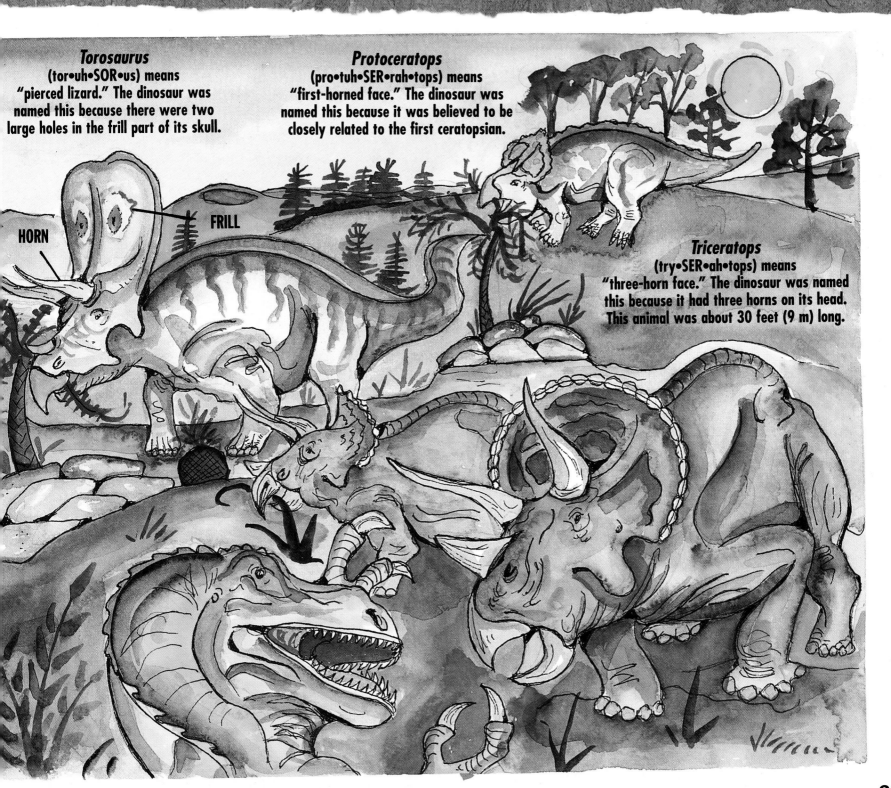

Torosaurus
(tor•uh•SOR•us) means "pierced lizard." The dinosaur was named this because there were two large holes in the frill part of its skull.

HORN

FRILL

Protoceratops
(pro•tuh•SER•rah•tops) means "first-horned face." The dinosaur was named this because it was believed to be closely related to the first ceratopsian.

Triceratops
(try•SER•ah•tops) means "three-horn face." The dinosaur was named this because it had three horns on its head. This animal was about 30 feet (9 m) long.

ORNITHOPODS

(OR·nih·thuh·pods) were the group of dinosaurs that usually had beaks or bills.

Ornithopods, which were plant eaters, used their beaks or bills to rip and tear their food. Some with very large heads had thick skulls with ornamentation. These dinosaurs were called boneheads. Some ornithopods had unusually shaped crests on their heads. Some had birdlike feet and stood on their hind legs most of the time. Some walked on all four. Paleontologists believe some of these dinosaurs lived in herds.

JURASSIC

BEAK

Dryosaurus
(dry•oh•SOR•us) means "oak lizard." The dinosaur was named this because it lived among trees. It was about 13 feet (4 m) long.

Lesothosaurus
(less•oh•tho•SOR•us)
The dinosaur was named for Lesotho, a city in South Africa, where it was found.

Boneheads probably had head-butting contests.

24

Edmontosaurus
(ed•mon•to•SOR•us) means
"Edmonton lizard." The dinosaur was
named this because its fossils were first
found near the city of Edmonton in Canada.

Lambeosaurus
(lam•bee•oh•SOR•us)
was named after Lawrence Lambe,
a famous paleontologist.
It had a head crest.

BILL

CREST

Corythosaurus
(koe•rith•uh•SOR•us) means
"Corinthian helmet lizard." The
dinosaur was named this because its
crest looked like a Greek Corinthian helmet.

Parasaurolophus
(para•saw•ruh•LOAF•us) means
"near crest." The dinosaur was named this
because the long curved crest on its head
was similar to that on another dinosaur
called *Saurolophus* (saw•ruh•LOAF•us).

Hypsilophodon
(hip•see•LOAF•uh•don) means
"hipsiloplus lizard." The dinosaur was named
this because its teeth resembled the teeth of a
lizard named *Hipsilophus* (hip•see•LOAF•us).

BONEHEAD

Stegoceras
(ste•GOS•uh•rus) means
"roof horn." The dinosaur was named
this because at first paleontologists
mistakenly believed the fossil was the
top of a horned dinosaur's skull.

Paleontologists believe dinosaurs had keen senses of sight, smell, and hearing. Most had eyes on either side of their heads so they could see all around them. Their ears were holes behind their eyes. They were constantly on the lookout for food or for the possibility of being attacked. Some paleontologists believe the crested ornithopods could communicate with sound. The crests were hollow and were attached to tubes inside their noses. When the crested onithopods blew air through the tubes, they might have been able to honk, bellow, or make trumpet sounds.

Paleontologists believe a *Tyrannosaurus* could smell its prey and anything else from a great distance.

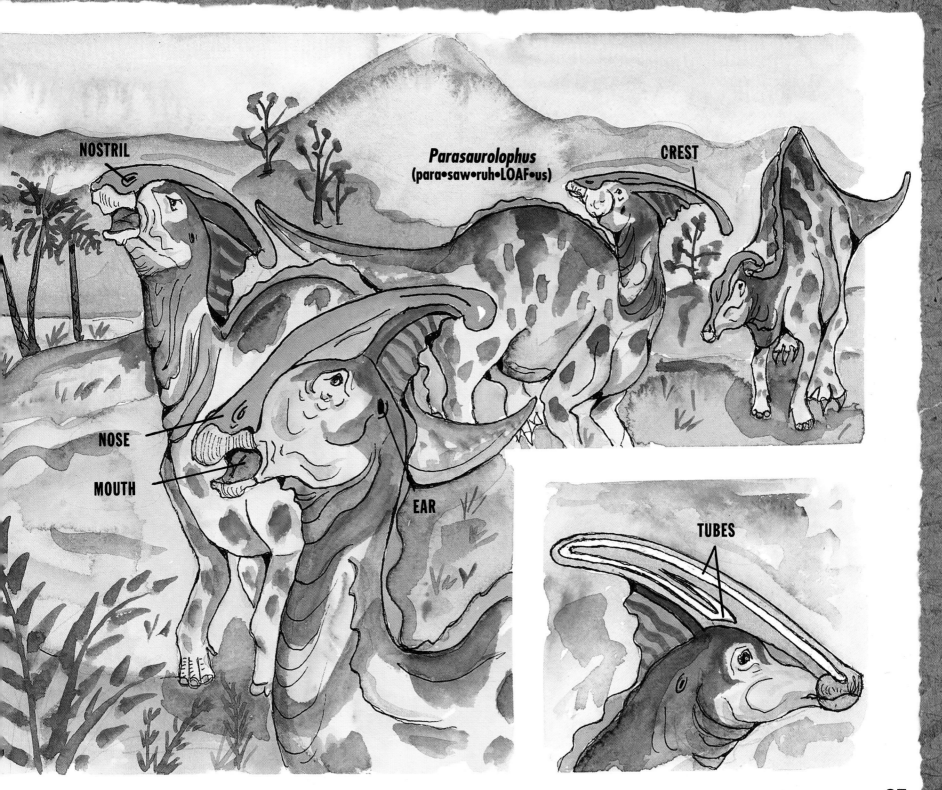

NOSTRIL

Parasaurolophus
(para•saw•ruh•LOAF•us)

CREST

NOSE

MOUTH

EAR

TUBES

27

Most female dinosaurs probably laid their eggs in soft, dirt nests. Some sat on their eggs, keeping them warm until they hatched. Other dinosaur mothers carefully covered their eggs for protection with plants, sand, and dirt, creating small mounds. The coverings also kept the eggs warm. When the eggs hatched, many kinds of hatchlings could live on their own right away. Still other dinosaur mothers took care of their young until the hatchlings were strong enough to live on their own.

In the 1920s, the first fossilized dinosaur nests were discovered in the Gobi Desert, in Mongolia, by an expedition from The American Museum of Natural History in New York City.

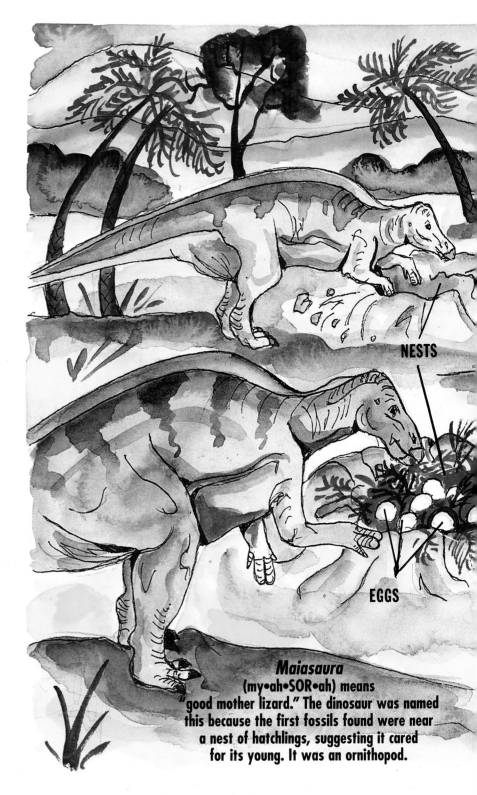

NESTS

EGGS

Maiasaura
(my•ah•SOR•ah) means "good mother lizard." The dinosaur was named this because the first fossils found were near a nest of hatchlings, suggesting it cared for its young. It was an ornithopod.

MOUND

HATCHLINGS

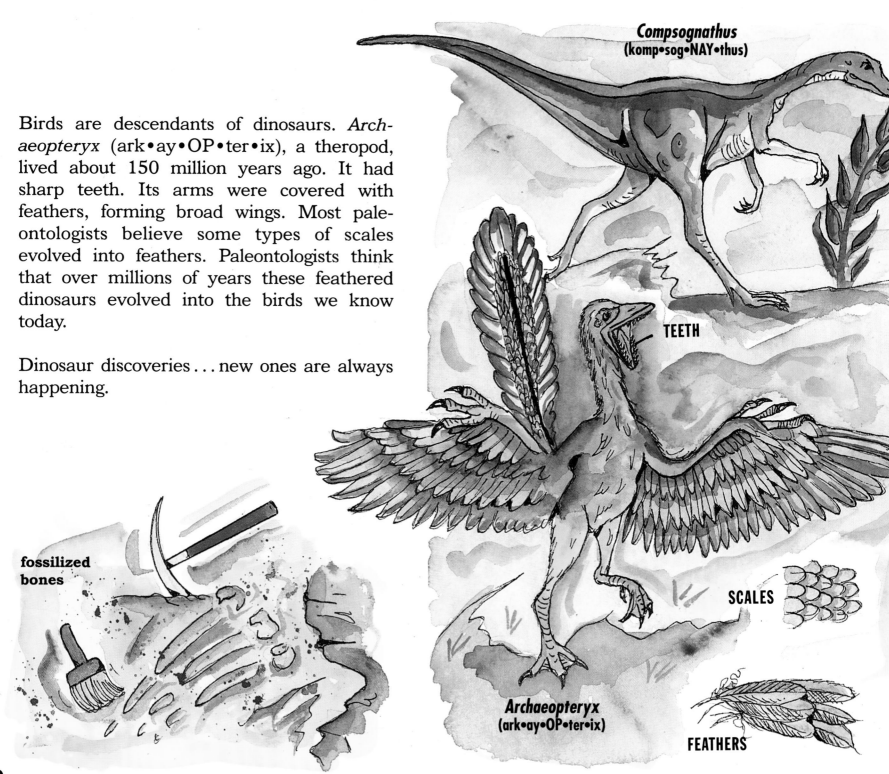

Birds are descendants of dinosaurs. *Archaeopteryx* (ark•ay•OP•ter•ix), a theropod, lived about 150 million years ago. It had sharp teeth. Its arms were covered with feathers, forming broad wings. Most paleontologists believe some types of scales evolved into feathers. Paleontologists think that over millions of years these feathered dinosaurs evolved into the birds we know today.

Dinosaur discoveries...new ones are always happening.

Compsognathus
(komp•sog•NAY•thus)

TEETH

fossilized bones

SCALES

Archaeopteryx
(ark•ay•OP•ter•ix)

FEATHERS

OSTRICH

WHOOPING CRANE

SPARROW

BLUE JAY

CARDINAL

MORE DINOSAUR DISCOVERIES . . .

Composognathus (komp•sog•NAY•thus), a theropod, was one of the smallest dinosaurs. It was only about 3 feet (1 m) long.

Coelophysis (seel•oh•FIE•sis), a theropod, may have eaten its own kind. Fossilized *Coelophysis* skeletons have been found with *Coelophysis* bones inside them.

Seismosaurus (size•mo•SOR•us), a sauropod, is believed to be the longest dinosaur that ever lived. It was about 164 feet (49.2 m) long.

The largest skeleton of a *Tyrannosaurus* (tuh•ran•uh•SOR•us), a theropod, ever to be found was 42 feet (12.6 m) long. It was discovered in South Dakota by a woman named Sue Hendrickson, so the fossilized skeleton was named Sue. It is on display at the Field Museum in Chicago, Illinois.

Gallimimus (gal•ee•MY•mus), a theropod, may have been the fastest running dinosaur. It is believed it could run about 40 miles (64 km) an hour.

Mamenchisaurus (mah•men•chi•SOR•us), a sauropod, is believed to have had the longest neck of any dinosaur, about 49 feet (14.7 m) long.

Dinosaurs that ate meat had very different-looking teeth than plant-eating dinosaurs. Those that ate meat usually had curved, blade-sharp teeth with sawlike edges. The plant eaters' teeth were odd-shaped and not as sharp.

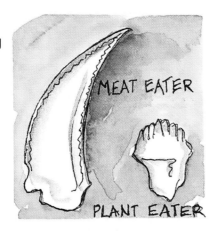

MEAT EATER

PLANT EATER

Titanosaurus (tie•tann•oh•SOR•us), a sauropod, left fossilized footprints, about 3 feet (.91 m) wide. The footprints are big enough to sit in.

Eoraptor (EE•oh•rap•tor), a prosauropod, means "dawn robber." *Eoraptor* lived at the beginning of the dinosaur era. A hunting dinosaur was often called a robber. *Eoraptor* is one of the oldest dinosaurs ever discovered.

DINOSAUR INDEX

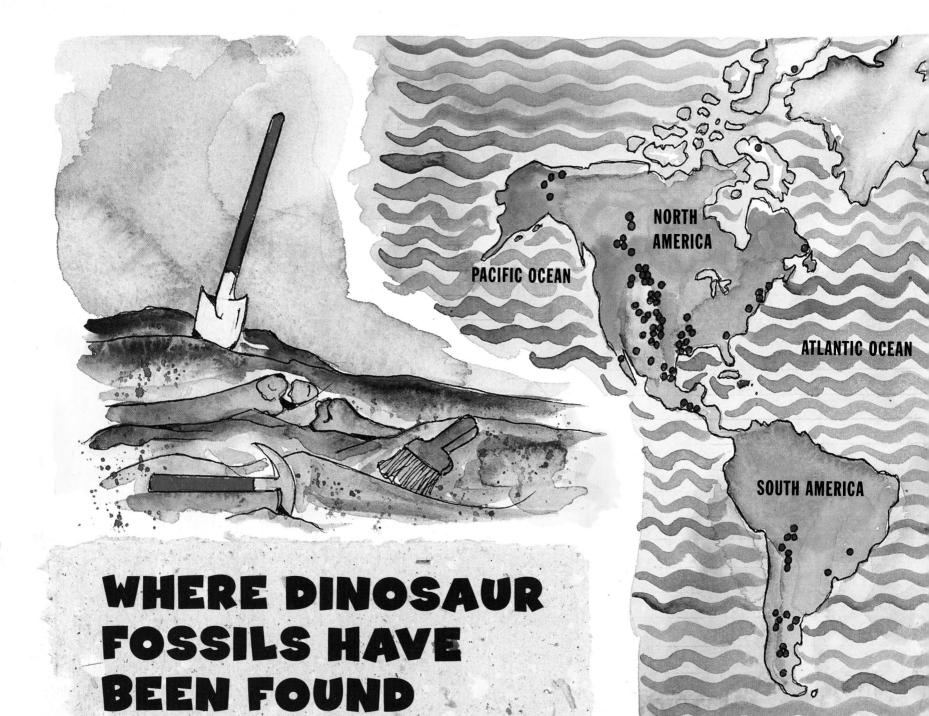

WHERE DINOSAUR FOSSILS HAVE BEEN FOUND